TO

FROM

DATE

BOB CARLISLE
BUTTERFLY KISSES™

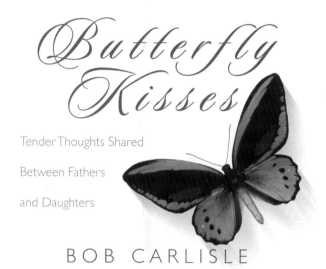

Butterfly Kisses

Tender Thoughts Shared

Between Fathers

and Daughters

BOB CARLISLE

COUNTRYMAN
®

BOB CARLISLE
BUTTERFLY KISSES™

Published by J. Countryman®,
a division of Thomas Nelson, Inc.,
Nashville, TN 37214

A J. Countryman Book

*Concept, design, and photography by
Koechel Peterson & Associates, Inc., Bill Tyler, Tom Henry,
Minneapolis, Minnesota*

ISBN: 1-4041-0093-8

Printed and bound in USA

How it all started

Several years ago, "Butterfly Kisses" was penned as a gift to my then sixteen-year-old daughter, Brooke. It was never intended for release by me or anyone else. I was sitting up late one night reminiscing and took out an old cedarbox full of photographs. As I began to look at the pictures of my daughter and me together, I came to the realization that I wouldn't have this child under my roof much longer. The song just poured out of me that night.

In addition to the newfound fame from the crossover success of "Butterfly Kisses," I've experienced a few interesting drawbacks, too. Like having truck drivers pull me over and good-naturedly threaten to slug me while pointing to dents in their trucks from running into something while listening to the song. (On the other hand, at least they're not expecting me to pay the repair bill.)

Then there are other reactions to the song that vary from incredibly moving to sometimes heartbreaking. I guess it's because certain stories reinforce something people already have and remind them of time's precious nature.

Unfortunately, it's also received by some folks who fantasize about what they wish they had in their lives. For instance, I get a lot of mail from young girls who try to get me to marry their moms. That used to be a real chuckle because it's so cute, but then I realized

they don't want a romance for Mom. They want the dad who is in that song, and that just kills me.

That's why I hope this book, based upon my song, becomes a bestseller. I want men to read the reflections of other men and their daughters and to see their relationship portrayed in pictures, in a way they can identify with. That way in the future they'll be inspired to create their own "Butterfly" memories with that special little girl in their lives. And if that happens, then the song and this book will have accomplished everything that I hoped they would.

Always hoping for your best, Bob

Bob Carlisle

*S*uccess has never eluded Bob Carlisle. The forty-year-old singer/songwriter has been in the music industry for over twenty years and has established a strong contemporary Christian following. In addition to having placed several songs on the Contemporary Christian top ten charts, he has written several others that have done very well by other artists on the Country chart.

Yet in spite of the success and notoriety Bob has enjoyed, even he was surprised by the phenomenal success and cross-over of "Butterfly Kisses." In fact, as he puts it, "My feeling was quite the opposite. We didn't pinpoint any specific market, and we're just watching this brushfire burn. Without trying to sound pretentious, it's all very humbling and means a lot to me. We didn't plan this—it just happened. It's almost like a grassroots thing out of the 1950s that I didn't think happened anymore in this country. It's great, and I'm enjoying it. But I have to admit it's a little strange to hear my song sandwiched between Eric Clapton and Smashing Pumpkins."

Unconcerned about trying to top himself, Carlisle remarks, "I write songs out of my own need and passion that always surrounds my family and don't see myself changing. I'll continue being as transparent as I can to my audience."

My necessity

When I first heard "Butterfly Kisses" I was amazed at the honor of having my father write a song just for me — and a song that so clearly overflowed from his heart. Even though my dad and I have always been close, this song has brought us even closer. Evidently it has had the same effect on fathers and daughters around the world.

My father is the most wonderful man in my life. He gives me never-ending love and friendship, which is a necessity in my life. Even when my dad is gone a lot on tour we still talk on an almost daily basis by phone — keeping each other updated on the specifics of our daily lives. My father is funny and fun to be around. Even when something has gone wrong he reminds me that no matter what happens he will always love me.

BROOKE CARLISLE

There's two things I know for sure

She was sent here from heaven

and she's daddy's little girl.

Walking in truth

When I reflect upon my daughter, Kelly, I think of strength and beauty. Her strength of character and will to succeed are inspiring to her dad. Her beautiful countenance reflects a heart of compassion that is tough and tender at the same time. As I watched her hold a young underprivileged child in her arms on a recent mission endeavor, I knew God had given the world someone very special. The smile I first saw when she was a toddler was now lighting the world. At that moment I bowed my head and gave thanks for the privilege of being Kelly's dad. I knew right then the greatest joy a Christian father can know. It is the joy of a child sharing your faith and walking in Truth.

JACK GRAHAM

Through the years

Dear Daddy,

Words can never truly express how much I love, appreciate, and admire you. Through the years you have taught me so many important lessons. When I was little you showed me how to ride a bicycle and taught me patience. When we moved and I was having a hard time adjusting, you taught me how to stick out the tough times. When I was having trouble with my math grades, you encouraged me to do my best. When I had to come home from college with mono, you showed me compassion. Your relationship with Mom has taught me faithfulness and how to have a successful marriage.

All those lessons were important, but teaching me about priorities was perhaps the most important. You always taught me Jesus first, others second, yourself last. You have taught me this mainly by being an incredible example. I love you so much, and I could never repay how much you have given me. I am truly proud to call you my dad.

Your loving daughter, Kelly

KELLY GRAHAM

A part of Meagan knows...

My daughter, Meagan, is eleven years old. She was born with cerebral palsy and very seldom shows any sentimental emotions. I was driving Meagan to school, and we were listening to KISS—FM radio station when the disc jockey, Kidd Kraddock, came over the radio and said that the next song was dedicated to all the fathers and daughters that were listening. I told Meagan to listen-up because this was going to be our song. About midway through the song I looked over at Meagan and her eyes started to tear up. I started getting very emotional. We were both crying while we were in rush-hour traffic.

As soon as Meagan got out of the car, I picked up the car phone and called my wife. I said, "Guess what— Meagan heard a song on the radio and cried!" You see, we along with the medical professionals are not sure if and when the different areas of her brain developed and which areas were damaged due to the trauma to her brain. Her reaction to the song let us know that there is a part of Meagan that knows what it feels like to be touched by something deep inside. Ever since we heard "Butterfly Kisses," I have felt a stronger bond with my daughter.

Good luck with your book and with all your future songs. It must be a neat feeling knowing that what you do makes a difference in so many lives.

ROBERT L. PIERCE

I was listening, Daddy

"Who gives this woman in marriage?" Usually a father will respond simply, "Her mother and I." Not my dad. The catch in his voice, the moistness of his eyes, the sweet, firm hug—those were special just for me. But we were in front of hundreds of people, which meant Dad's one line in my wedding was another chance to tell everyone What's Really Important.

"Kathy was brought here by her family and friends, her church and her God. I have the honor to speak for all," he said, then hugged me and formally entrusted me to my dear husband, Greg. All the people at the wedding were part of bringing me to that moment on my life's journey, and Dad was reminding us how important we all are to each other every day.

Dad is in heaven now, in perfect companionship with all the saints, and his gentle wisdom means even more to me. Because of him, my relationships are richer and each moment holds more holiness. And someday when I'm reunited with him, I'll testify that although my journey to heaven was made possible by Jesus, it was made splendid by relationships with my family and friends, my church and my God—and my dad.

14

As I drop to my knees by her bed at night, she talks to Jesus, and I close my eyes.

And I thank God for all of the jo

in my life,

But most of all, for...

Dad's special hug

One of the blessings in my life is my father. One thing that makes my dad so special is his hug. Whether it is to congratulate me after a triumph or comfort me after a fall, it always tells me that he loves me. There is just something about his hug that says it doesn't matter what you have done or what you will do, I will always love you. My dad is my encourager, leaving me little notes saying how much he loves me. He's my number-one fan, always there to cheer me on in everything that I do. I am so blessed to have both a heavenly Father and an earthly father who love me.

NATALIE JEFFREY

No one else can call me "Daddy!"

One of the greatest joys of my life was holding my baby daughter right after she was born. To realize I had a daughter, to understand that I was a daddy. What makes it so special to be the daddy of a girl? Maybe—the way she calls me *Daddy*! No one else in the world can call me that. It is also the incredible way she says it.

It was the unique way she fit on my shoulder when I rocked her to sleep every night as an infant. It was the way she ran to me and jumped into my arms when I walked in the house at the end of a long day, hearing her scream, "Daddy's home!"

It is the way she is growing up into a beautiful, godly young lady who loves Jesus, loves life, and loves her daddy.

What a blessing it is to be a daddy to a daughter!

NEAL JEFFREY

Butterfly Kisses after bedtime prayer

Stickin' little white

flowers all up in her hair.

A prayer for happiness

My daughter, Kari, was pregnant with her second child and unexpectedly went into premature labor. She was only nineteen weeks along, and we all knew it would take a miracle to save her unborn child. She spent sixty-four days in the intensive care unit. Kari called me one night, sobbing and asking me to pray for her. She had lost her appetite and felt miserable.

I remember praying that she would wake up the next morning happy and hungry. She had forgotten the prayer, and the next day she was excited to tell me how she had eaten five bowls of cereal and really felt happy. In a few days she said, "Dad, keep praying for me—but only to be *happy*, not *hungry*. I've gained five pounds!"

GARY SMALLEY

My first date

I remember my first date with my dad like it was yesterday. I was six years old, and I put on my best dress and my mom curled my hair. As I waited excitedly for him to escort me to the car, I ended up dashing to the bathroom and throwing up! I was so worked up, my brothers kept saying to me, "What's the big deal? It's just Dad."

As a young girl, I cherished those "Daddy's dates" because I had his undivided attention. He didn't read a newspaper while we waited for our food, but listened attentively to my every word. One date we had when I was thirteen years old he helped me plan a husband-to-be list. To this day I have the list and a husband that is everything I ever dreamed of on that very date with my dad.

I'm all grown up now with two children of my own, but I still look forward to my special dates with my dad. I'm proud to admit I don't throw up anymore, but I still get those excited butterflies inside.

KARI SMALLEY

"Walk beside the pony daddy,

"I know the cake looks funny daddy, but I sure tried."

Daddy, can't we please take it home?

We promised Andrea and Sara desks for their rooms. Sara was especially enthused. When she comes home from school, guess what she does? She plays school! I never did that as a kid. I tried to forget the classroom activities, not rehearse them. Denalyn assures me not to worry, that this is one of those attention-span differences between genders. So off to the furniture store we went.

Andrea and Sara quickly succeeded in making their selections. Somewhere in the process Sara learned we weren't taking the desks home that day, and this news disturbed her deeply. I explained that the piece had to be painted and they would deliver the desk in about four weeks. I might as well have said four millennia.

Her eyes filled with tears. "But Daddy, I wanted to take it home today."

"Daddy, don't you think we could paint it ourselves?"

"Daddy, I just want to draw some pictures on my new desk."

"Daddy, please let's take it home today."

After a bit she disappeared, only to return, arms open wide and bubbling with a discovery. "Guess what, Daddy. It'll fit in the back of the car!"

The clincher, though, was the name she called me: "*Daddy*, can't we please take it home?"

The Lucado family took a desk home that day.

I heard Sara's request for the same reason God hears ours. Sara wanted what I wanted for her; she only wanted it sooner.

Sara's request was heartfelt.

But most of all, I was moved to respond because Sara called me "Daddy." Because she is our child, I heard her request. Because we are his children, God hears ours.

Oh, with all that I've done wrong

Turning to my dad

Mom was the one I went to with any problems. This changed after the unexpected death of my mother last year. Suddenly I found myself turning to my dad, at first for comfort and then later for understanding. Soon my dad was helping and advising me with all those problems and questions that a person faces when they are making life-changing decisions.

Dad has taught me that these decisions don't need to be the mountains that we sometimes make of them; but when they are, sometimes the best thing to do is smile and start up the slope. Now I often regret the fact that I didn't include my dad very much when I was growing up. Perhaps if I had, those terrible teenage years would have been a bit more ascendable.

While the circumstances are unfortunate, I am so glad that I got the chance to have a strong and loving relationship with my father!

JONI BERGSTROM

To deserve a hug every morning,

And Butterfly Kisses at night.

Sweet sixteen today,

She's looking like her momma

a little more every day.

One part woman, the other part girl

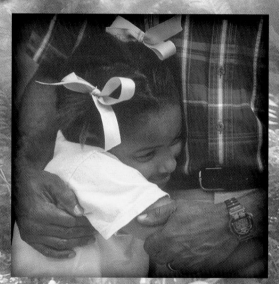

To perfume and makeup,

from ribbons and curls.

Trying her wings out in a great big world

But I remember...

Butterfly Kisses...

after bedtime prayer.

Stickin' little white flowers all up in her hai

Sickin' little white flowers all up in her hai

You know how much I love you daddy
But if you don't mind

I'm only going to kiss you
on the cheek this time."

She gave me strength

I have a little seventeen-month-old daughter, Dekala. Early in her life I was locked up in a penitentiary. I was able to visit with her only on the weekends. Every Sunday night I would cry because of the things I had done to be apart from my beautiful daughter. It was hard, but she gave me strength!

When I was released I cried with her. Now, I'm not a very sentimental man. I listen to Oldies and Rap. Her mother heard the song ("Butterfly Kisses") and bought it for me. As soon as the second chorus started I was crying, just because it was so beautiful and it was my life!

R. D. OSMUND

With all that I've done wrong,
I must have done something right.

Unconditionally yours

Your mother and I have tried to instill in each of you God's truth. Chrystal, my firstborn, I love you dearly. I remember well your growing-up years—how you used to hug me when I came home, how you refused to go to sleep unless we rocked you first. Even then you often refused to let us leave you. I also remember the groundings I had to give you because you went where you weren't supposed to go. Some of those teenage years were tumultuous.

Well, you're grown up now, and I'm proud of you. I'm proud every time I see you leading the choir, and I'm proud when you tell me of the things you're learning. I pray for you when I hear of your struggles regarding your career plans.

God has given you a keen mind and sensitive spirit. Please use this special ability to lead others always in the path of righteousness.

Thank you for helping your mother and father learn the meaning of family. I love you unconditionally, and I will lift you before God's throne in prayer every day of my life.

DR. TONY EVANS

Anytime... anywhere

When I think about my dad, I have so many good memories. He always felt it was important to be there for us. When we had to be picked up from school, he would come for us even if that meant conducting a meeting in the car with us in the back seat. Daddy insisted on coming to eat lunch with us periodically in high school, even though we were often embarrassed. He always showed up at my track meets, and his was the single voice I heard as I crossed the finish line.

I think the fondest memories I have of him are the family vacations he planned every year. On our cross-country drives, we would start out at midnight. Daddy would drive all night. He and I would be the only ones up sometimes. I'd be up reading, and he'd be driving and listening to tapes.

CHRYSTAL EVANS

To deserve her love every morning

All the precious time
like the wind, the years go by.

Precious Butterfly

And Butterfly Kisses at night.

Spread your wings and fly.

My "Sugars"

We had called the baby "Suzanne" months before her birth, and when I saw her I couldn't speak a word—she was just right! I was on the road a lot, but my "Sugars" was always ready to crawl up in my lap (her favorite place to watch television) and then have me carry her to bed, read to her, pray with her, and then scratch her back until she was asleep.

As I watched her go to school her very first day, I knew things would never be the same. I remember flying once from Philadelphia to Portland on one tour and figuring a way to fly through Dallas to see her perform in her first play. When we left her at the dorm in Missouri for college, I thought I could not make it. I filled her car with gas before we left town, and to this day I dislike that gasoline station.

She fell in love with the "special one" for her life, and I knew my "Sugars" would never be the same—nor would we. Walking her down the aisle, my eyes were so full of tears I could hardly see. As she glowed, she turned to me and said these words which I'll never forget, "Daddy, it will be all right—don't cry." Precious and few are the moments I treasure with my precious daughter.

"BIG" JOHN HALL, *Gospel Singer*

The gentle giant

Being a mother instantly changes your outlook on life. Your view becomes somewhat skewed. I have finally fallen into the cliché, "When you are a parent, you will understand…." As I look at my husband with my son, I am reminded of the significance of "father."

It is truly a special bond.

My father and I always had this special bond. He has a pet name for me, and only he uses it—"Sugars." It has always been special between the two of us. There were things my father did that (now as a parent) I look upon not only with great fondness, but deep understanding.

My father has touched me mostly with his sentimentality. To look at this man with such a large frame, "sentimental" would be the last word one might use to describe him. Trust me…he is a gentle giant! I was always crawling up in his lap, and as long as I can remember he carried me to bed. A tear is often seen in his eye when he is moved by something, and he isn't afraid to say, "I love you, Sugars." As I walked down the aisle on my wedding day, I saw those tears—not so much for sadness, but a feeling of overwhelming love and pride. I love my dad, and yes, now I understand.

SUZANNE HALL STEWART

She'll change her name today.

and I'll give her awa

She'll make a promise,

Standing in the bride room

just staring at her,

she asked me what I'm thinking, and I said, "I'm not sure."

Dear Dad

When I was a little girl
I wouldn't go to sleep
Until you came and scratched
    my back
And sang some songs to me.

When I was very sick
And had to stay home for months,
The highlight of my day
Was when you'd come home
    for lunch.

When I was in high school
    you got transferred
And I begged you to let us stay,
So you commuted more than
Four hours every day.

I know that you didn't have
The best childhood

So you made ours the greatest.
You did all that you could.

You worked so hard
To get where you are today.
You even survived three
    teenage daughters
Who look up to you in every way.

Dad, this year I'll get married
And I'll get my degree,
And through all these changes
You've been here for me.

My plans for the future
Include being close to Mom and you
Because I'll need your advice
If I become a parent, too.

Your loving daughter.

"I just feel like I'm losing my baby girl." Then she leaned over and gave me...

An intimate invitation

My beautiful, twenty-one-year-old daughter, Shelly, was a bridesmaid when I performed my son's wedding. It was such a sentimental moment that Shelly, tears welling up in her eyes, had to turn her face away from me as she took her turn down the aisle. After the ceremony she reassured a relieved father that she could never handle me performing her wedding.

Two years later, in the middle of a moving ceremony performed by a friend of mine for his daughter, my wife leaned over and whispered, "By the way, Shelly's decided she wants you to do her wedding after all." Despite the shock, I was thrilled. After fifty-one years I may have become jaded to many things — beautiful sunsets, fresh dogwood blossoms, or even a snowy winter's morn — but what dad isn't brought to his knees by such an intimate invitation from his own, admiring little girl.

BYRON WILLIAMSON

He's my hero

My dad has always been a source of encouragement and emotional support for me. He's my hero. He's my friend. And he's always been in love with my mom.

Dad challenges me to live and become. In his efforts to let me go and let me feel the chill of adulthood, I've only come to realize how much I need him, how much I depend on his reassurance and friendship when I feel afraid and uncertain.

I witnessed his God while growing up. Now He is my God, and I share this faith with my dad. He did it right.

"I'm proud of you." "I love you." "You're the prettiest when you smile." I've heard my dad say these a zillion times. He's always pursued friendship with me. He's always made me feel valuable. He's always made me feel like no matter what happened, no matter how bad things got, he would love and support me. His example is a living testimony to me.

SHELLY WILLIAMSON

Butterfly Kisses, with her momma there

Sticking little white flowers all up in her hair

"Walk me down the aisle daddy,

it's just about time."

"Does my wedding gown look pretty daddy?"

"Daddy don't cry."

The perfect song

My dad's name is Steve Simmons. He is forty-six years of age. My dad is such a strong man today. So strong that I can't remember seeing him cry or even hearing about him crying. Until one Tuesday afternoon.

The phone was ringing as I walked through my door after a long day at work. I picked up the phone. It was my mom. She said, "Turn on KDWB. That 'Butterfly Kisses' song is on next." Then she hung up. Soon after the song was over, my phone rang again, and it was my dad. He said, "Would you like to dance with me to that song at your wedding?" I was so shocked, and I could not stop crying. My dad has never been the emotional type.

Then he asked if I cried when I heard the song. I said, "Yes, this is the perfect song for us." Then my dad said that *he* cried also. I was so happy and so shocked that I did not know what to say except, "I love you, Dad!" That song will always remind me of that day.

ANDREA SIMMONS

With all that I've done wrong

I must have done something right.

To deserve her love every morning,

And Butterfly Kisses....

I couldn't ask God for more,

Man, this is what love is.

Daddy's little girl

I am getting married on August 9.

I am the youngest of eight children, which made me "Daddy's little girl," and I loved every minute of it. He would make me my favorite sandwiches for lunch, even if it meant making two different sandwiches. And he would always joke around with me, looking under the table to make sure I didn't waste any of his good cooking!

When I was in fifth grade I left home to catch the bus, hugged and kissed my dad, and said, "I love you, like always." That day, during my spelling test I got called down to the office. My uncle was standing there. He got me, and we went to get my brother and sister from the junior high, and we went home. My dad had died.

My youngest older brother will be giving me away at my wedding. We will have a rose on the altar for my dad, but the song would make it all the more special.

LINDA McDOWELL

I know I've gotta let her go,

but I'll always remember...

My Two Butterfly Kisses

Though as distinctive as sugar and salt, Amy and Holly both add spice to each tasteless encounter offered by life.

I recall the evening I watched the Atlanta Braves play a game on TV that went into extra innings. The game was over around 3:30 a.m. I had planned on going fishing the next morning, as I did every Friday. Amy heard me as I headed out the door and insisted on going to keep me awake as I drove one hour to my favorite spot.

With Holly, it was the time she sang in school with an alternative band and asked me to work with them in preparing THEIR music. I was indeed honored.

Sugar and spice and everything nice—that's my girls!

MICHAEL W. BURT

Every hug in the morning

And Butterfly Kisses...

A word from the publisher

I hope this book based on Bob Carlisle's
song "Butterfly Kisses" becomes one of your most
cherished possessions, and that it inspires you to
live and appreciate every moment to its fullest —
especially those golden "Butterfly Kisses" moments
shared with your children and loved ones.

Time is fleeting. It only
comes in moment-to-moment increments.

It's those special moments shared
with your loved ones that make life worth living
and that time can never take away.

May God grant you love, joy, peace, happiness,
good health, and an abundance of "Butterfly Kisses."